TAKING ACTION ON CLIMATE CHANGE

DYING OFF
Endangered Plants and Animals

ALEX DAVID

New York

Published in 2020 by Cavendish Square Publishing, LLC
243 5th Avenue, Suite 136, New York, NY 10016

First Edition

Website: cavendishsq.com

Library of Congress Cataloging-in-Publication Data

Names: David, Alex, author.
Title: Dying off : endangered plants and animals / Alex David.
Description: First edition. | New York : Cavendish Square, 2020. | Series: Taking action on climate change | Audience: Grades 5 to 8. | Includes bibliographical references and index. |
Identifiers: LCCN 2019017925 (print) | LCCN 2019019092 (ebook) | ISBN 9781502652331 (ebook) | ISBN 9781502652324 (library bound) | ISBN 9781502652317 (pbk.)
Subjects: LCSH: Bioclimatology--Juvenile literature. | Nature--Effect of human beings on--Juvenile literature. | Endangered species--Juvenile literature. | Extinction (Biology)--Juvenile literature. | Climatic changes--Juvenile literature.
Classification: LCC QH543 (ebook) | LCC QH543 .D38 2020 (print) | DDC 577.2/2--dc23
LC record available at https://lccn.loc.gov/2019017925

Copy Editor: Nathan Heidelberger
Associate Art Director: Alan Sliwinski
Designer: Ginny Kemmerer
Production Coordinator: Karol Szymczuk
Photo Research: J8 Media

The photographs in this book are used by permission and through the courtesy of:
Cover, Marten_House/Shutterstock.com; p. 4 Bettmann/Getty Images; p. 10 avh.de (http://www.avh.de/en/stiftung/name nspatron/portrait.htm)/Alte Nationalgalerie/File: Alexandre humboldt.jpg/Wikimedia Commons/Public Domain; p. 12 Image extracted from page 150 of The American Centenary; a history of the progress of the Republic of the United States during the first one hundred years of its existence, by LOSSING, Benson John. Original held and digitised by the British Library. Copied from Flickr (https://www.flickr.com/photos/britishlibrary/11113478075)/File: LOSSING(1876) p150 OSWEGO STARCH FACTORY, OSWEGO, NY (T. KINGSFORD & SONS).jpg/Wikimedia Commons/Public Domain; p. 15 Harry C., Own work/File: Carbon-cycle-full.jpg/Wikimedia Commons/CCA-SA 3.0 Unported; p. 18 Education Images/UIG/Getty Images; p. 22 David Evison/Shutterstock.com; p. 25 Tom Stoddart/Hulton Archive/Getty Images; p. 26 Melanie Stetson Freeman/The Christian Science Monitor/Getty Images; p. 29 © Ardea/Fink, Kenneth /Animals Animals; p. 31stevegeer/E+/Getty Images; p. 33 Aditya Singh/Moment/Getty Images; p. 34 ALEXANDER GRIR/AFP/Getty Images; p. 36 Andy Nelson/The Christian Science Monitor/Getty Images; p. 39 MLADEN ANTONOV/AFP/Getty Images; p. 40 No machine-readable author provided. Chensiyuan assumed (based on copyright claims)/File: Bison herd grazing.JPG/Wikimedia Commons/CCA-SA 3.0 Unported; p. 42 Evelyn Hockstein/ Washington Post/Getty Images; p. 46 Paul Souders/Photolibrary/Getty Images; p. 47 iStockphoto.com/ChoochartSansong; p. 49 Elizabeth W. Kearley/Moment/Getty Images; p. 50 SDB/ZOJ/Sheri Determan/WENN/Newscom; p. 52 HervÃ© de Gueltzl/Photononstop/Getty Images; p. 53 Ben Osborne/The Image Bank/Getty Images; p. 55 iStock/undefined undefined.

Printed in the United States of America

Portions of this book originally appeared in *Adapting to Plant and Animal Extinctions* by Kathy Furgang.

CONTENTS

Jane Goodall interacts with a chimpanzee in Gombe National Park.

Introduction

When Jane Goodall was ten years old, she decided she'd like to leave her home in England and go to Africa so that she could live with the animals. Sixteen years later, in 1960, when Goodall was twenty-six years old, she did exactly that. She went to Tanzania and studied chimpanzees.

Louis B. Leakey mentored Jane Goodall as she researched and made fascinating discoveries about animal societies. She walked through the forests in low Converse sneakers, observing chimpanzees. She saw that they used tools, fought in wars, had compassion, and treated their infants similarly to how human parents treat their own babies. Goodall fell in love with these animals. Leakey remarked that based on Goodall's discoveries, "We must now redefine man, redefine tool, or accept chimpanzees as human!"

Through her years of research, Goodall realized that chimpanzees were at risk. In a 2003 TED talk, Goodall told the audience the chimpanzees in Gombe National Park in Tanzania were in danger. Hunters now had roadways into forests that allowed them to travel back and forth between animal habitats and cities easily. They shot any animals they saw for bushmeat, then smoked and dried the meat, drove back into the city centers, and sold it. The animals Goodall had studied—those sophisticated primates with complicated cultures—were at risk of becoming endangered.

There are four countries in Africa where chimpanzee populations have already disappeared. In 1900, there were 1 million chimpanzees living in the wild. In the twenty-first century, there are fewer than 340,000.

In 1977, Goodall founded the Jane Goodall Institute. This organization works all over the world, helping animals and the ecosystems that they live in. As Goodall researched animal populations, she began to realize that animals could not be saved until the humans who live near them are first helped. In Gombe, Goodall saw many people who were discouraged about the threat of climate change. Their farmland was overused and infertile. They could not grow food to support themselves. Goodall's organization works to help communities of people find sustainable solutions so that then they can in turn support the animals that live around them. Goodall thinks you must help people in order to help animals.

The Human Animal

As we begin to talk about animals being endangered, it must first be remembered that humans and animals are not two distinct ideas. Humans are animals. Humans are part of the animal kingdom. They are mammals, just like bears, lions, or sea otters. Mammals are defined as creatures that have fur, nurse their young with milk, have three bones in their middle ear, and have one single bone on each side of their jaw. Humans are not only mammals, but also primates. Classified under the category "great apes," humans are also called "hominins." The humans that live today are called *Homo sapiens*. They share 98 percent of their genes with chimpanzees.

Humans and other animals share an interconnected relationship. Humans not only influence animals, but animals also influence us. The human animal has caused widespread changes to Earth's climate—most significantly because of carbon emissions. Amazingly, animals can help reduce these carbon emissions. Later, we will investigate the ways animal habitats can actually reduce the carbon output that is responsible for the rising temperatures of global warming.

Systems Thinking

Climate scientists and biologists often think of animals and humans using a systems-thinking approach. Earth is one large ecosystem that contains many smaller ecosystems. Within this global system, humans happen to be an apex predator, just like wolves and lions. However, we also appear to be an invasive species. In 1819, there were fewer than 1 billion people on Earth. By 2019, there were 7.7 billion people. In order to sustain our way of life, we have taken over land and put it to use for our own habitat, so that we may feed and house our growing species.

As we expand, we need more and more to feed and sustain us. We have created what Tom Wessels calls "the myth of progress." Wessels's theory is that humans believe we can expand infinitely, without any serious repercussions. Humans think we can continue to use large amounts of carbon and grow and grow and grow. However, according to Wessels, the laws of natural, complex systems will not permit this. We must look to other systems—like forests, for example—in order to understand how to make real, sustainable progress. In the twenty-first century, we are realizing that, like the creatures in a forest, we need to live in balance with other species.

Perhaps at our worst, humans arrogantly think that we are more evolved than the plants and animals around us—that we don't need to live in balance with nature. We can consume and spread over more land and take more, without any consequences. However, we are now realizing this is not the case. There are between 5,400 and 5,500 species of mammals worldwide. Between 2005 and 2013, one-fifth of the great ape population (not counting humans) diminished. Gorilla populations are declining by 3 percent every year. Humans must be the stewards of our ecosystem. In the words of Jane Goodall, "I wanted to come as close to understanding animals as I possibly could." It is up to us—and up to us *now*—to prevent both the extinction of our animal cohabitants and to prevent the extinction of humanity.

This is a portrait of Alexander von Humboldt from 1806.

CHAPTER 1

The Truth About Climate Change

Scientists around the world acknowledge that the climate is changing. One of the ways our climate is changing is that Earth is getting warmer. In the twenty-first century, we are experiencing global warming.

Global warming is not a new concept. In 1800 and again in 1831, Alexander von Humboldt was the first person to identify the possibility that humans were causing Earth's atmospheric and oceanic temperatures to rise. Traveling through Latin America in 1799, Humboldt began to think about isotherms, the differences in temperature and pressure on weather maps. During a hike up an inactive volcano in Ecuador, Humboldt recorded observations of plants and animals. He began to understand that humans, plants, and animals are all interconnected and affected by each other. He saw that the disturbances of humans could cause major problems for other species. The atmosphere is sensitive and could easily change because of humans.

In the twenty-first century, we are thinking about climate change in this same way. However, we now have more research, more tools, and more science to understand what is happening to our Earth because of our own actions.

What Is Climate Change?

Climate change is variations in Earth's atmospheric and oceanic temperature, wind and weather patterns, and other changes in climate. It is not simply the weather changing. Weather is

During the Industrial Revolution, factories and trains began to rely on fossil fuels to produce and transport goods.

temperature and precipitation changes that happen day to day, whereas climate occurs over a longer period of time—decades or centuries.

Scientists can see that our climate has changed since the end of the eighteenth century, when humans began to change from an agrarian to an industrial way of life. This was the onset of the Industrial Revolution, a time when nations such as the United States and Great Britain began to invent ways to get work done with machinery instead of by hand. The end of the eighteenth century and the beginning of the nineteenth century saw a huge increase in the number of factories. The factories made goods faster, cheaper, and more easily than ever. Steam-powered factories could work around the clock. Steam-powered trains transported goods to locations throughout newly industrialized nations. The burning of coal created the steam that powered all this heavy machinery.

A revolution had begun. More people began working in factories than on farms. Soon, gasoline-fueled cars were manufactured on assembly lines and became easier and cheaper to produce. Over the years, more families were able to buy cars. They could now travel faster and more comfortably than with a horse and carriage, so car sales climbed higher and higher. People saw the Industrial Revolution as progress. In many ways, it certainly was progress and made our lives much easier. However, there were also drawbacks to this new Industrial

Revolution. These drawbacks took a bit longer for people to recognize than the obvious benefits.

The factories, machines, electricity, and transportation all required the burning of fossil fuels. A fossil fuel is a resource extracted from the ground that has taken a very long time to form. Coal and petroleum are examples of fossil fuels. Coal has formed over millions of years from the remains of once-living organisms. Burning coal provides the energy needed to run a factory, heat a home or business, and provide electricity to cities or towns. At the beginning of the twentieth century, fossil fuels were being burned and consumed in large quantities for the first time. When fossil fuels are burned, they release pollution and noxious gases into the air. This has always been apparent when looking at old factories and mills from the early twentieth century. The black smoke and pollution released into the air only increased over the years.

The introduction of the automobile on a large scale only made things worse. Gasoline, which is made from petroleum, is another fossil fuel that is burned and releases pollution into the atmosphere. Just one hundred years ago, there were not even enough paved roads to connect every town in the United States. Today, many families own more than one car, and highways become jammed for miles due to the high volume of traffic.

Scientists say that it is the burning of fossil fuels that has caused the overall increase in temperatures over the century.

Why? Because within the pollution released by the burning of fossil fuels are so-called greenhouse gases. These gases include carbon dioxide, water vapor, methane, and ozone. It is the increase in carbon dioxide that scientists are singling out as the single greatest contributing factor to the climate-change problem that our planet is experiencing.

The Carbon Cycle

Carbon dioxide is a natural gas that occurs in the atmosphere. In fact, you release carbon dioxide out of your body every time you exhale your breath. It is a waste gas that is produced naturally by animals after they process the oxygen their bodies need. Meanwhile, trees and other plants use carbon dioxide to

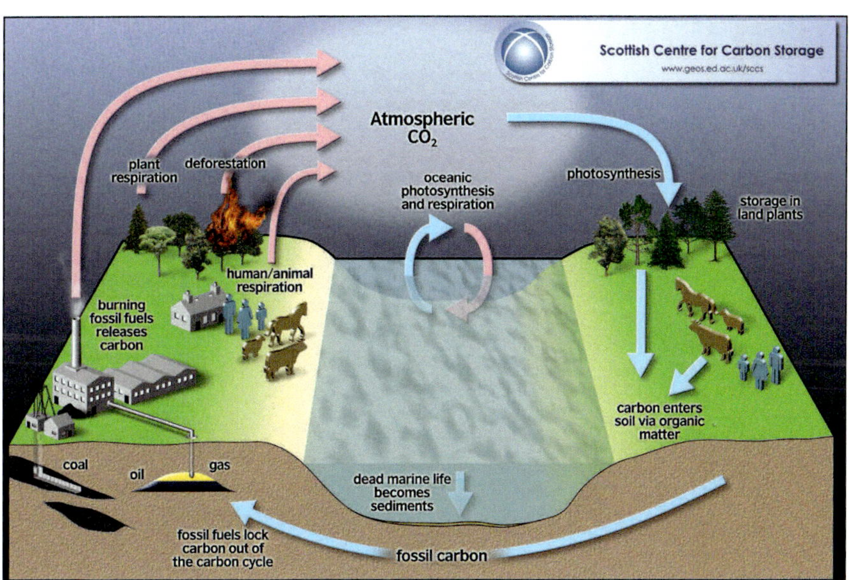

A diagram of the carbon cycle is shown above.

drive photosynthesis. Plants couldn't survive without the carbon dioxide in the air. This natural flow of carbon dioxide through the environment is called the carbon cycle.

If it's already a natural part of the environment, what makes the carbon dioxide produced by burning fossil fuels so dangerous? Scientists say that it is the unnaturally large amount that has accumulated in the atmosphere over the past century. Large-scale burning of fossil fuels is a human activity that had not existed before the past two centuries, and that is the same period of time in which global temperatures have been increasing steadily and fairly dramatically. Scientists have found that carbon dioxide and other greenhouse gases are accumulating in the atmosphere and creating a virtual blanket over the atmosphere. The blanket traps heat, much like the sun's heat becomes trapped under the panes of glass in a greenhouse.

The greenhouse effect is natural and even necessary. It is what makes the planet temperate enough to be habitable. If the sun's heat were not trapped in the atmosphere, the planet would be far too frigid to support life. It is the excessive buildup of these greenhouse gases, however, caused primarily by the burning of fossil fuels, that is causing global warming and resulting in climate change.

Scientists have been keeping temperature and climate data for over a century, and they have also been looking ahead to predict what effect our current activities will likely have on the changing climate in the future. Mathematical climate models were invented in the 1950s and have improved greatly over the decades. Today's models take into account the effects that air circulation over oceans has on the climate. When this data can be input into a computer model, scientists can figure out the mean overall temperatures for certain areas around the globe. These models can also take into account different scenarios for future levels of carbon dioxide and greenhouse-gas emissions.

In a 2018 analysis, the Intergovernmental Panel on Climate Change (IPCC) reported an increase in global temperatures of about 1.8 degrees Fahrenheit (1 degree Celsius) since the mid-1800s. The IPCC suggests that the temperature is rising about 0.4°F (0.2°C) every ten years. This may sound like a very small amount. However, the amount is quite significant over such a relatively short period. In addition, it is an average, overall temperature increase worldwide, which means that some areas have seen a greater increase. Scientists have been able to attribute the increase in global temperatures to the increase in carbon dioxide emissions. They have noticed a direct correlation between the increase of carbon dioxide in the atmosphere and the increase in Earth's global surface and ocean temperatures.

Humans' Negative Impact

The effect of human activity on plant and animal extinction is not a new story. Human activity has affected plant and animal life throughout history. When humans build towns and cities, plant and animal habitats are destroyed. Trees are leveled, and paved roads run through the ecosystems that animals rely on for food. If a plant species in an area is already suffering or endangered, construction and development projects may wipe the organism away entirely. One example of human-influenced extinction involves bird populations.

Richard Duncan, a professor at the Institute for Applied Ecology, was able to look at bird populations throughout the Pacific Islands region. He determined that human colonization caused 1,300 species to become extinct. That's 10 percent of

Here is a colony of albatrosses that live on Midway Atoll, an island in the North Pacific Ocean.

POACHING

In addition to climate change, animal populations also suffer because of poaching, or hunting animals for profit. Elephants have been the victims of poaching. In the early 1800s, there were ten million elephants. In the twenty-first century, there may only be five hundred thousand elephants left. Thirty thousand African elephants are killed by poachers every year for their tusks, which poachers sell to stores and factories that make goods out of them.

In 2017, a public awareness campaign helped create a ban against the ivory trade in China. Basketball player Yao Ming served as the face of the campaign. China had been one of the world's largest markets for ivory. After the country's government made it illegal to sell ivory, around two hundred ivory shops and factories closed. This shows that public awareness and government action may be key to repopulating species like elephants.

the total population of birds on Earth. Bird populations in the United Kingdom are also suffering. From 1966 to 2012, the UK bird population declined by about forty-four million. These are concerning statistics for our global ecosystem.

The Future Planet

One of the most important international organizations studying the problem of global warming and climate change is the United Nations World Meteorological Organization (WMO). The WMO has 192 member states and territories. Each contributes to a cooperative study drawn from observation sites on land, at sea, and in space. The data that is collected helps to refine computer climate models that can better predict how global temperatures will change over the next several decades.

In 1988, the WMO created the Intergovernmental Panel on Climate Change (IPCC). Every five to seven years, the IPCC reports on the state of Earth's climate. The IPCC uses the knowledge of thousands of scientists and researchers to report on climate change. It is divided into three working groups, each with a specific task. For instance, Working Group III is tasked with understanding how to mitigate, or make less painful, the effects of climate change. In 2021, the IPCC will report on its sixth assessment cycle. In 2018, the IPCC and the Conference of Parties (COP) created a special assessment to prepare countries for the effects of Earth reaching 2.7°F (1.5°C) above pre-industrial levels.

One key finding of the report is that Earth has already warmed about 1.8°F (1°C) since the start of the Industrial Revolution, and it is already experiencing changing weather, rising sea levels, and the melting of glaciers as a result. Therefore, humans must do everything in their power to limit Earth's temperature increase to 2.7°F (1.5°C). Global warming affects plants and animals. Warmer weather means changes in habitat and changes in diseases. As the planet warms, there are many threats to plants and animals.

A green sea turtle lays her eggs on a beach at night.

CHAPTER 2

Threats to Plants and Animals

As humans adapt to climate change, their own survival solutions sometimes cause harm to animal and plant ecosystems. For instance, if a city is at risk of flooding, building a seawall may protect the city, but it may also destroy sea turtle habitats. It is essential that as humans try to save themselves from the effects of climate change, they also take into account the effect of their actions on plants and animals. In order to help save animals and plants, we must first acknowledge the problems we are facing. We will do this by defining some key terms.

Defining the Terms

We use the terms "extinct," "endangered," and even "threatened" when we talk about the status of different species. What do these terms mean? The most severe of these terms, of course, is "extinct." This means that there is no more of that particular species left on Earth; the species is gone forever. Every last organism of its kind has died off worldwide.

An endangered species is at risk of extinction throughout all of its range or a large portion of its range. There are currently more than sixteen thousand plant and animal species that are considered endangered. Each year, the Red List, a list of species that are in danger, grows. Created by the International Union for Conservation of Nature (IUCN), it is the most comprehensive benchmark of how plants and animals are faring. Zoos, governments, and scientists are a few of the groups that use the IUCN's information to try to help plants and animals. The Red List classifies plants and animals into seven categories. They are the following: least concern, near threatened, vulnerable, endangered, critically endangered, extinct in the wild, and extinct. In 2019, 27,150 species fell into the vulnerable, endangered, or critically endangered categories. Those species included 40 percent of the world's amphibian species, 34 percent of conifer species, 33 percent of reef corals, 25 percent of mammals, and 14 percent of birds.

According to the World Wildlife Fund, some of the animals that were considered critically endangered in 2019 were the

A black rhino walks in Zimbabwe's Mana Pools National Park.

Amur leopard, black rhino, Bornean orangutan, Cross River gorilla, eastern lowland gorilla, and hawksbill turtle.

A threatened species is one that is in danger of being added to the endangered list. An animal may be listed as threatened in a particular range or throughout the world. While human-driven habitat destruction is the main reason why so many animals and plants are on the endangered and threatened species lists, humans can also do a lot to help these animals return from near extinction. In the United States, for example, the gray wolf population has been able to increase sufficiently to be removed from the country's endangered species list. One thing that has helped has been the Endangered Species Act of 1973. This US law made it a crime to kill any plant or animal on the endangered species list. Humans have also been prevented from developing areas where endangered plants and animals live.

With the negative effects that climate change brings, the struggle of threatened and endangered species gets even harder. Their conservation will become even more important in the coming years as the effects of climate change become more severe.

What Climate Change Means for Plant and Animal Ecosystems

In the twenty-first century, if humans do little to change their carbon emissions, Earth will continue to heat up, although it won't heat up evenly. Some regions will heat up more than others.

Photographed above is a bird mural that passersby can see as they walk around New York City.

BIRD MURALS

In New York City, art and conservation meet in colorful murals of endangered birds. The National Audubon Society and the Gitler & _____ Gallery have collaborated by asking artists to paint 314 bird species threatened by climate change. In 2014, the National Audubon Society wrote a report examining the impact of climate change on North America's birds. They found that more than 50 percent of the continent's bird species are threatened by the warming climate. This mural project allows city dwellers to see exactly what these birds look like. The murals create a harmonious mix of the urban environment and elements of the avian world, which allows passersby to wander, wonder, and consider helping these at-risk bird species.

Scientists at the UCAR Center for Science Education state that during the twenty-first century, the temperature is predicted to rise between 3.2°F (1.8°C) and 7.2°F (4.0°C). The distribution of temperature change will vary. Air over land will heat up more quickly than air over water. Higher latitudes will heat up more than mid-latitudes. These changes can have devastating effects on the organisms in these regions.

Mountain Species

In a 2018 study by the University of British Columbia, zoologists found that for every 1.8°F (1°C) rise in Earth's temperature, species of animals that live in mountain habitats will move up the slope 328 feet (100 meters). Global warming makes their habitats too warm to be livable, so they must move to find cooler temperatures. This means moving up the mountain. Because of this, their habits are growing smaller and their populations are declining. One animal species that is affected by this is the northern pocket gopher. This animal lives in Nevada's Ruby Mountains. In the past eighty years, a 2°F (1.1°C) temperature increase drove populations to cooler locations.

Warmer temperatures also affect plants. The alpine meadow flower found in the Himalayas has lost 29 percent of its habitat and moved up into elevations that are about 2,000 feet (600 m) higher due to warming temperatures.

Above is a photograph of a northern pocket gopher.

Invasive Species

Alternatively, some species may thrive under the new warm temperatures, although this may not be a good thing. Nonnative plants better acclimated to new climate conditions may begin flourishing. That means they will be invading new areas where they had never lived before. In some ways, this means an increase in biodiversity in a region. However, the invasive species can have very negative and unpredictable effects upon food chains. According to the National Wildlife Federation, about 42 percent of the threatened or endangered plant and animal species in the United States are at risk because of invasive species in their environment.

Invasive plants can be a large problem for an ecosystem. Seeds may end up in a new environment in several ways. Often, migrating animals bring seeds with them that are then relocated and germinate in new territory. These seeds often travel after being stuck to the fur of some animals or being eaten and excreted as waste by animals. If the invasive seeds germinate and the resulting plants grow quickly and crowd out native plant species, an imbalance in the food web may occur.

Not only do invasive plant and animal species cause extra competition for resources in an area, they may also spread disease or attack the native species in some way, preventing them from reproducing. Even bacteria and fungi can become invasive in an area, just like plant and animal species. Many bacteria and fungi thrive where the temperature is warmer. For this reason, more and more of the planet is becoming hospitable territory for them as global temperatures rise. The consequences can be catastrophic to vulnerable species.

In 2018, the Peru stubfoot toad was assessed by the IUCN. That year, its population was decreasing, and it was labeled as "critically endangered." The Red List stated three reasons for its population decline: pollution of its grassland environment, hunting, and threats because of an invasive species.

Trophic Cascades

The term "trophic cascade" refers to changes in the flow of energy or food within an ecosystem. Each ecosystem has lots

A wolf is an apex predator.

of different parts reacting to each other. For instance, wolves are a top, or apex, predator in an ecosystem. They eat deer and elk. However, when wolves are depopulated from an area, the elk and deer populations increase. This creates damage to the entire ecosystem because the deer or elk consume too many plants. The ecosystem becomes overgrazed. This then affects the homes of songbirds and butterflies. Therefore, wolves actually make life easier for birds and insects.

A trophic cascade can have either a top-down or a bottom-up effect. A shortage of wolves creates a top-down effect. They are the apex predator in a system, and thus, when their populations change, the bottom of the ecosystem is affected. However, a plant like kelp or an organism like a coral can have a bottom-up effect. When kelp or corals are diminished, they affect the rest of the ecosystem because there is not enough food for larger animals.

Biodiversity

In 1985, Professor Edward O. Wilson coined the term "biodiversity." It is short for "biological diversity." Biodiversity is the idea that an ecosystem has lots of different living parts to it. Biodiversity has many levels, and variation allows for our whole planet to work better.

Biodiversity is important for an ecosystem because we are all responding and reacting to each other. On a very simple level, there would not be oxygen in the air if we didn't have plants and forests changing carbon dioxide into the oxygen we breathe. Within a forest, there is also a lot of biodiversity. For instance, in 25 acres (10 hectares) of forest on the island of Borneo, there are seven hundred species of trees. We also need animals in forests to eat fruit and move the seeds of trees around, thus repopulating the forest.

Biodiversity is essential for human life. As plant and animal species become endangered or extinct, biodiversity is threatened. Tiger populations decreased by 97 percent between 1918 and 2018. Conservationists are worried about how humans are causing biodiversity to dwindle. In 2011, a global treaty was created by the Convention on Biological Diversity (CBD).

In Ranthambore National Park in India, three wild tigers walk together. Tigers are an endangered species.

It laid out goals for 2020. One was that 17 percent of all land and 10 percent of all oceans should be protected.

Professor Wilson, in his landmark paper on biodiversity, says, "This being the only living world we are ever likely to know, let us join to make the most of it." His words ring true as we begin to understand how interconnected we are. Each of our decisions creates a reaction in our natural world. Interestingly, the natural world may be able to help us with the problem of global warming more than we think.

Displaced and hungry polar bears find food in a garbage dump in a remote part of Russia.

CHAPTER 3

Affected Plants and Animals

So far, we have discussed some of the reasons why plants and animals are threatened. Now, some examples of threatened animals will be discussed. It is important to save species, to create better habitats, and to make all poaching illegal so that animals and plants survive and thrive. In saving animals, we are also helping our own survival. There are many animals that create a positive effect in lowering carbon emissions. This means that saving threatened animal species is essential to saving human habitats as well.

Polar Bears

Polar bears are on the IUCN Red List as "vulnerable." They live on Arctic ice, and that ice is melting due to global warming. Polar bears don't have the room to breed or hunt. If no action is taken against global warming, polar bears are likely to become extinct by 2100.

Additionally, humans are also interfering with the survival of polar bears because of governmental decisions. In 2017, a Republican bill in the United States opened the Arctic National Wildlife Refuge, a place where many polar bears live, to oil and gas development. President Donald Trump and his administration wanted to use the land to drill for oil and refill the 800-mile (1,300 km) Trans-Alaska Pipeline System.

Dr. J. Alan Pounds researches golden toads in the Monteverde Cloud Forest.

The Golden Toad

The last time scientists saw the golden toad species was in 1989 in the Monteverde Cloud Forest of Costa Rica. It is now extinct, although there is some disagreement in the scientific community about how the species became extinct.

Scientists like J. Alan Pounds, a biologist at the Monteverde Cloud Forest, believe that global warming caused the toad's extinction. Humans emitted huge amounts of carbon into the atmosphere, and this caused Earth's temperatures to rise. This caused rain forests, like the Monteverde Cloud Forest, to become hotter and drier, which allowed the chytrid fungus to thrive. It attacked the golden toads and killed them.

However, other scientists, like Kevin Anchukaitis and Michael Evans from the University of Maryland, believe that the forest changed because of El Niño. El Niño is a weather pattern in the Pacific Ocean that affects temperatures and rainfall in North and South America. These scientists believe that El Niño caused dry temperatures that allowed the fungus to spread.

Either way, the golden toad species, an important part of the Monteverde Cloud Forest ecosystem, is now extinct.

The Yakutian Horse Lowers Carbon Emissions

The Yakutian horse lives above the Arctic Circle and can survive temperatures of –100°F (–73°C). Father and son scientists Sergey and Nikita Zimov are the directors of a place called Pleistocene

ALDO LEOPOLD

Many think of Aldo Leopold as the father of wildlife conservation. Leopold was an American who lived from 1887 to 1948. He was a great lover of nature, spending his childhood near the Mississippi River. He often thought about nonliving parts of an ecosystem. Later in his life, he came up with the idea of the "land ethic." This is the idea that we should care for the land when we think about ecosystems. He believed that conservation is a harmonious interaction between humans, animals, and the land. The land, which contains both biotic (living) and abiotic (nonliving) features, is vital for a healthy ecosystem.

Park in the Mammoth Steppe, a region of the Russian Arctic. Permafrost covers 45 percent of this part of the Arctic. It stores about 1.4 trillion tons (1.27 trillion metric tons) of carbon. As the Earth is warming, the permafrost will melt and carbon and methane will be introduced into the atmosphere as greenhouse gases. If global warming reaches 3.6°F (2°C), the emissions from the melting permafrost will increase global warming even more. However, when the Yakutian horses eat the grasses, they remove the snow on top of the permafrost. The snow insulates

Yakutian horses run with one another over the cold snow.

the ground, so when the horses remove the snow, it makes the ground colder, so the permafrost stays cold. The Zimovs want to repopulate the Mammoth Steppe with animals. They believe that thirteen thousand years ago, before the end of the ice age, hunters killed fifty species of large mammals. These mammals, the wooly mammoth for instance, became extinct. When these mammals left this ecosystem, the other fauna and flora left too.

This is an example of a trophic cascade. The environment relies on herbivores, like the Yakutian horse, to keep the ecosystem healthy. Therefore, it is not only important to save animals so that they may survive, but also so that our greater systems may survive. By fostering the survival of the Yakutian horse in the Arctic, we are indirectly preventing carbon emissions from entering the atmosphere.

American Bison

In the early 1800s in America, tens of millions of bison were in the American West. From 1850 to 1900, these animals became nearly extinct because of big game hunting. Private ranchers like Charles Goodnight and a powerful government figure, President Theodore Roosevelt, saved the species by allowing the bison refuge on ranches and by creating the American Bison Society. The bison began breeding, and their populations grew. However, now biologists are concerned that the American bison is genetically not the same animal. During this time of

Bison graze together in a field.

conservation, the bison bred with cattle, thus changing their genome (DNA).

In 2009, James Derr wanted to save the American bison's genome. He wanted to make sure the genes of the American bison were not contaminated with cattle genes. To do this, he wanted wildlife managers to make sure pure herds didn't mix with herds that have cattle genes. In his efforts, Derr used fourteen loci, or patterns in the genetic code, to identify if the bison had cattle genes. He worked on creating an "SNP chip," a test that would be able to quickly tell what proportion of the bison genome had cattle genes.

Some conservationists disagree with Derr. They believe that a bison is a bison and the individual genes should not make a difference. However you feel about genetic purity, Derr's work creates complexity in identifying which animals are actually bison and which are a hybrid. This could change classifications in the Endangered Species Act. Some bison may qualify as endangered.

As we can see, there are many threats to plants and animals. Luckily, many humans are concerned about losing biodiversity and losing animals that may help offset our carbon crisis. Zoos and conservation organizations are working to protect animals and plants that may be in danger of dying off.

The Smithsonian Conservation Biology Institute breeds dama gazelles, shown here in 2014.

CHAPTER 4

Conservation Efforts

You may think that conservationists should put all their effort into saving individual species on the Red List. Although there are efforts to save individual species, many conservationists take the approach of saving the entire ecosystem. By making sure the land, the plants, the apex predators, and the prey are all in harmony with one another, more species can be protected. In doing this, conservation efforts take many forms.

Zoos work directly with teams of scientists in the habitats where species are in danger. They work with the public to educate them about forest birds in Hawaii and iguanas in the islands in the Atlantic. They study the African wild dog in Zambia to see how it is adapting to its environment. The National Zoo in

Washington, DC, helps teach farmers in Africa how to prevent the spotted cheetah from ruining their crops without resorting to hunting. The Houston Zoo is working on saving the tapir in Venezuela, where it is endangered due to habitat loss and human activity.

Cutting-edge technology is also helping scientists learn about species and the ways they are adapting to the changing climate. This growing body of knowledge is helping bring some endangered species back from the brink of extinction.

Monitoring Systems

Scientists know that the best way to monitor animals in their natural habitat is to do it without being detected. Since observing animals in the ocean is extremely difficult to begin with, remote video monitoring and satellite technology are great tools for observing ocean ecosystems.

Remote monitoring systems are ideal for scientists because they allow observation of the animals in a truly natural environment. The tools also provide records that can be collected over time and studied alongside data from other populations. As with other environmental studies about climate change, the remote satellite monitoring of species may take several years to produce useful data that can help scientists draw important conclusions about climate change. It is these conclusions that can help to make policy changes to safeguard the environment and provide financial support for further study of climate change.

Drones

Drones are also proving to be useful for researchers and scientists. In 2018, scientists Serge Wich, Alex Piel, and Fiona Stewart from Liverpool John Moores University used drones to create conservation data for chimpanzees in Tanzania, Africa. Before drones were being used, researchers had to travel on foot to track chimpanzees. This proved to be quite difficult, as chimpanzees are extremely active. They may move across 19 to 27 square miles (50 to 70 square kilometers) over a year on the hunt for food. It is also hard to track these animals because their habitat includes a lot of hills, and there are not many roads for cars. Additionally, chimpanzees create nests that are sometimes 147 feet (45 m) above the ground. Drones seemed like a much more logical solution.

The small motorized cameras take photos of chimpanzee nests. The researchers then count the nests and estimate how many chimpanzees are living in a given area. Researchers create large data maps that use coordinates to show where each nest is located. As drone technology gets better, their conservation efforts will also improve. The researchers later experimented with thermal imaging options on the cameras and found that it was much easier to count individual chimpanzees than estimate with nests. Drones indicate that new forms of technology may help us protect animal species.

A drone, pictured above, can monitor animals without interfering with their habitat.

Cloning Endangered Species

Cloning has not yet taken off as the preferred method of preserving endangered species, but it is becoming a part of our daily reality. In 2019, scientists in Indore, India, took tissue cultures from rare and endangered trees to create clones. The scientists cut branches from the trees that are endangered—the *sagon*, *kadam*, and *paadar* trees—and then took their buds to their lab to reproduce the cultures. The scientists are hopeful that their experiment will help repopulate threatened tree species.

Using Traditional Conservation Methods

Because scientific technology develops and changes over time, we will soon have more ways than ever to save endangered plant and animal species and to adapt to the inevitable extinctions of some of these organisms. Until then, however, scientists are working hard to use traditional conservation methods to save threatened and endangered species. These methods involve preserving land for plants and animals to live on without the disruption of human activity. Wildlife preserves are areas set aside for the flourishing of ecosystems and food webs with a minimum amount of human interference or impact.

Another way that scientists and conservationists preserve species is by breeding endangered species in protected environments that exist apart from predators and human development. Following successful breeding, the animals are then reintroduced to the natural environment so they can live on their own without further human assistance. This was done for the bald eagle, which was close to extinction just a generation ago. The animal's habitat had been largely destroyed by humans. It had been hunted to the point of extinction because it was viewed as a threat to livestock. Even more damage was done to the bald eagle populations by a pesticide called DDT, which was first widely used in the 1940s. It caused the birds to lay eggs with shells that were too thin to survive until the babies hatched.

A *kadam* tree farm is pictured above.

ELEPHANT ORPHANAGE

The government of Botswana is concerned about African elephants. Out of all the countries in Africa, Botswana has a relatively high elephant population, about fifty thousand. An organization called Elephants Without Borders (EWB) is trying to help keep those numbers up, both by encouraging reproduction in elephant populations and by caring for hurt animals. Based in Kasane, Botswana, EWB has created the Elephant Orphanage. Similar to Jane Goodall's mission of helping the people in an ecosystem in order to help the animals, the Elephant Orphanage employs local Botswanan people. They are often under the age of twenty-five years old. This gives jobs to the local population of humans and allows them to learn animal husbandry skills so that the elephant population may continue to thrive. One calf, Molelo, was rescued from a bush fire. Another was airlifted from a different part of Botswana (near the border of South Africa) when he got caught in a farmer's fence. The elephants are cared for and nursed back to health.

Laws were put in place banning both hunting and the use of DDT. Nesting sites were protected so that the greatest number of eagles would be able to hatch. It took many years before populations of bald eagles returned in large enough numbers for

The bald eagle, photographed above, is a conservation success story.

the species to be removed from the endangered list. The return of the bald eagle is a success story that scientists wish would be the outcome of every conservation effort they attempt.

The bald eagle is a hopeful sign that humans can help reverse the effects of climate change, poaching, and habitat destruction. Conservation is a key part of revitalizing animal and plant species. Biologists, researchers, and scientists can change our planet, but ordinary individuals can also help. There are many ways that we can change our daily habits to reduce carbon emissions. We can lobby governments to change policies that would negatively impact ecosystems. We can join organizations and connect with other people who are interested in creating a healthier Earth. It is not just adults that can do these things, but also young people like you.

Members of Jane Goodall's Roots and Shoots organization hold up peace doves at the Los Angeles Zoo and Botanical Gardens in 2018.

CHAPTER 5

Now What?

In Jane Goodall's work to protect animals in Africa, she noticed that the people she met seemed like they had lost hope. Their land was infertile. It had been overfarmed. They were struggling. She knew that the animals would not be saved unless she could help the community of people. She began an organization called Roots and Shoots. Roots and Shoots is an organization which helps people in communities organize and positively impact the environment. In her words, "Every single day we live, we can make a difference, and together, with everybody making a difference, we can change the world." Here are examples of things you can do, organizations you can get involved with, and the psychology of habit change that is meant to inspire you to follow in Goodall's footsteps and make positive actions that benefit our entire global ecosystem.

Reduce Your Carbon Footprint

When everyone becomes aware of the causes of climate change, we can work to prevent the problem from growing. Reducing your carbon footprint means changing your behavior to lower the amount of greenhouse gases put into the atmosphere because of your daily activities. This can mean using alternative energy sources that are renewable, such as solar or wind energy. It can mean using cars that use alternatives to gasoline, such as electric hybrid vehicles. It can also mean driving only when needed or taking public transportation, biking, or walking whenever possible. Even turning off the lights in your home or using electricity and electrical devices only when needed can help you dramatically reduce your carbon footprint (not to mention your electricity bill).

Riding your bike is a way to reduce your carbon footprint.

Many nations and corporations have made pledges to reduce their carbon emissions over time. If individuals and families did the same, then the population as a whole would be more environmentally aware and responsible. As the human population increases and developing nations begin to require and consume more energy and resources, it is even more necessary for people to use no more than what they need. Scientists agree that the reduction of greenhouse gases in the atmosphere is the only way to reduce the overall effects of climate change.

Become a Volunteer

Some local branches of wildlife organizations have programs that young people can get involved in. Cleaning local parks, wildlife areas, lakes, and shorelines helps make ecosystems safe for animals and makes soil healthy for plants to grow in.

Volunteers help to clean up an oil spill in Wales that has affected this bird's ecosystem.

ROOTS AND SHOOTS

Founded by Jane Goodall in 1991, Roots and Shoots is an organization and a movement that encourages young people to take action, be empathetic to all living beings, and work together to make the world a more hospitable place for both human animals and nonhuman animals.

Roots and Shoots empowers young people to become the leaders we need in order to help reduce climate change. It encourages young people to join groups, create action plans, and network with other young people around the world. It uses social media and local community meet-ups so that young people can be the change they want to see in the world.

Sometimes, ocean communities are faced with oil spills that affect birds, water animals, and plant life. Volunteers often help to clean these oil-coated animals and return the environment to a healthy condition in which animals can thrive again. Even picking up trash along a beach can help protect a seashore's animal and plant communities.

Starting a school club or group that raises awareness of endangered species and climate change is a good way to help out. Raising awareness can help change behaviors and get more people involved in taking care of the planet.

Support Environmental Legislation

It is important to be informed about how local, state, and federal politicians feel about environmental issues. When they support legislation that will protect the environment or help slow the effects of climate change, people have to be aware of it, express their approval of pro-environment laws, and support the election and reelection campaigns of pro-environment candidates. Find out where leaders stand on the issues and consider supporting the ones that vow to be most helpful for the environment.

Be Aware of Invasive Species

Invasive species can cause ecosystems to be greatly damaged. They have even caused the extinction of some plant and animal

Zebra mussels, pictured above, are an invasive species in the United States.

species. Be aware of species that do not belong in an ecosystem. Plant only native plants in your yard or garden, and remove invasive plants from your property. Report any new species of plants or animals that you have never seen before in your area.

When camping, use firewood only from the area you are camping in. Many insects and their eggs travel in firewood and are introduced to a new area when the wood is relocated. Insects can cause damage to an ecosystem by competing for resources with native species. When they do not have natural predators in the area, they tend to take over and cause an imbalance in the food web and ecosystem.

Hope

In the words of Dr. Jane Goodall, "You have to decide what kind of difference you want to make." Every one of us is formed by a series of actions, hopes, and ideas. We can be the catalysts for the future, the agents of change that reverse the negative effects of climate change and create better ecosystems for plants and animals. Earth is one big system, and humans are an influential part of it. Together, we can choose to make our environment our top priority. Each day, we can take part in a series of small actions that will allow all animals—humans and nonhumans—to live harmoniously together on this great, big, beautiful planet.

Glossary

biodiversity The variety of life in any ecosystem or area.

carbon footprint The amount of carbon dioxide released due to the activities of a nation, state, community, group, or person.

climate model A computer simulation that uses current data to predict future climate conditions over a period of time.

cloning Creating a genetic replica of an organism made from the cells of that organism.

ecosystem A biological environment consisting of all the organisms living in a particular area, as well as all the nonliving, physical components of the environment.

emission The production or release of something, such as a gas.

endangered In terms of plant and animal species, being in imminent danger of becoming extinct.

global warming A long-term increase in average global surface and ocean temperatures, largely as a result of human activity; a key driver of climate change.

greenhouse gases Gases, particularly carbon dioxide and methane, that contribute to the greenhouse effect by trapping heat in Earth's atmosphere.

hominins A classification of animals that includes humans and their ancestors.

isotherms Markings on a weather map that indicate differences in temperature and pressure.

poaching The illegal killing of animals for profit.

threatened In terms of plant and animal species, being vulnerable to endangerment in the near future; in danger of becoming extinct.

Further Information

Books

Clinton, Chelsea, and Gianna Marino. *Don't Let Them Disappear: 12 Endangered Species Around the Globe*. New York, NY: Philomel Books, 2019.

Grolleau, Fabien, and Jérémie Royer. *Audubon: On the Wings of the World*. London, UK: Nobrow, 2016.

Rhodes, Wendell. *Threatened, Endangered, and Extinct Species*. New York, NY: PowerKids Press, 2017.

Wild, Paula. *Return of the Wolf: Conflict and Coexistence*. Madeira Park, BC, Canada: Douglas & McIntyre, 2019.

Websites

Animal Planet Endangered Species
http://www.animalplanet.com/wild-animals/endangered-species
This website allows viewers to learn about endangered species through articles and videos.

IUCN Red List of Threatened Species
https://www.iucnredlist.org
This website lists the threat status of many species.

US Fish and Wildlife Service Endangered Species
https://www.fws.gov/endangered
This website allows readers to check their own state for endangered species.

Organizations

Elephants Without Borders (EWB) Affiliate Office
500 Linwood Avenue
Buffalo, NY 14209
United States
(716) 884-1548
Website: http://elephantswithoutborders.org
Elephants Without Borders aims to preserve elephant populations.

The Jane Goodall Institute
1595 Spring Hill Road, Suite 550
Vienna, VA 22182
(703) 682-9220
Website: http://www.janegoodall.org
The Jane Goodall Institute is an organization committed to preserving and protecting great apes.

Roots and Shoots
1595 Spring Hill Road, Suite 550
Vienna, VA 22182
(703) 682-9220
Website: https://www.rootsandshoots.org
Roots and Shoots is a website and Facebook group that allows young people to connect with one another and take action to help the environment.

World Wildlife Fund for Nature (WWF)
1250 24th Street, NW
Washington, DC 20037
(800) 960-0993
Website: http://wwf.panda.org
The WWF promotes a harmonious relationship with nature by creating sustainable energy resources, encouraging biodiversity, and challenging wasteful consumption.

Selected Bibliography

"Climate Change Is Making Our Environment 'Bluer.'" *U.S. News & World Report*, April 7, 2011. http://www.usnews.com/science/articles/2011/04/07/climate-change-is-making-our-environment-bluer.

"Climate Change May Impact Extinction Risk of Animal Populations: Study." *International Business Times*, April 6, 2011. http://www.ibtimes.com/articles/131113/20110406/climate-change-environment-global-warming-animal-populations-spectral-colour.htm.

Conniff, Richard. "How Species Save Our Lives." *New York Times*, February 27, 2011. http://opinionator.blogs.nytimes.com/2011/02/27/how-species-save-our-lives.

Dilthey, Max Roman. "Examples of Organisms Endangered Due to Invasive Species." *Sciencing*, March 2, 2019. https://sciencing.com/examples-organisms-endangered-due-invasive-species-18813.html.

Eisenberg, Cristina. *The Wolf's Tooth.* Washington, DC: Island Press, 2010.

Gerstein, Julie. "11 Extinct Animals We've Lost in Our Lifetime." *Popular Mechanics*, October 1, 2015. https://www.popularmechanics.com/science/animals/g201/recently-extinct-animals-list-470209.

"Global Warming Pushing Alpine Species Higher and Higher." *ScienceDaily*, September 10, 2018. https://www.sciencedaily.com/releases/2018/09/180910093526.htm.

Goodall, Jane. "What Separates Us from Chimpanzees?" Filmed March 2003. TED video, 27:21. https://www.ted.com/talks/jane_goodall_on_what_separates_us_from_the_apes.

"Greenhouse Ocean Study Offers Warning for Future." *U.S. News & World Report*, May 19, 2011. http://www.usnews.com/science/articles/2011/05/19/greenhouse-ocean-study-offers-warning-for-future?s_cid=related-links:TOP.

Hawken, Paul. *Drawdown: The Most Comprehensive Plan Ever Proposed to Reverse Global Warming*. New York, NY: Penguin Books, 2018.

Kusnetz, Nicholas. "Save the Animals, Save the Planet?" *Inside Climate News*, August 15, 2016. https://insideclimatenews.org/news/14082016/save-animals-planet-extinct-species-carbon-dioxide-atmosphere-climate-change-global-warming.

"Mapping Chimps: Drones and the Future of Conservation." *AAG Newsletter*, February 4, 2019. http://news.aag.org/2019/02/mapping-chimps-drones-and-the-future-of-conservation.

Reed, Stefan. "American Oystercatcher." National Audubon Society, July 31, 2017. https://www.audubon.org/news/american-oystercatcher-stefen-reed.

Richardson, Valerie. "Trump Administration Steams Ahead with Plans to Open Alaska's ANWR to Drilling in 2019." *Washington Times*, December 20, 2018. https://www.washingtontimes.com/news/2018/dec/20/trump-open-arctic-national-wildlife-refuge-oil-dri.

"What Is the Difference Between Endangered and Threatened?" US Fish and Wildlife Service. Retrieved September 2011. http://www.fws.gov/midwest/wolf/esastatus/e-vs-t.htm.

Index

Page numbers in **boldface** refer to images.

About the Author

Alex David has her MFA from New England College. She has a chapbook coming out with Dancing Girl Press called *Animals I Have Loved*. Her poems and short stories have been published in literary journals such as *Green Mountains Review* and *Adelaide Literary Magazine*. Additionally, she has taught a class on eco-fiction at Canisius College in Buffalo, New York. She loves to learn and write about climate science. She is hopeful for the future.